TIME, TIDE <u>AND</u> PLACE

A COASTAL FLY FISHER'S CHRONICLE

PHOTOGRAPHS & FISHING REPORTS

Ted Hendrickson

To Charlie
Fair Winds - Tight Lines!

Ted Hendrickson   16 June 2006

FLAT HAMMOCK PRESS

All inquiries should be addressed to:

The Publisher, Flat Hammock Press, 5 Church Street, Mystic, CT 06355

www.flathammockpress.com   860-572-2722

FIRST EDITION

Library of Congress Cataloging-in-Publication Data

Hendrickson, Ted.
    Time, tide, and place : a coastal fly fishers chronicle : photographs
and fishing reports / Ted Hendrickson.
        p. cm.
    ISBN 0-9773725-0-2
        1. Landscape photography--New England. 2. Fly fishing--New England.
    3. Hendrickson, Ted. I. Title.
    TR660.5.H44 2006
    779'.3674--dc22

                                        2006003289

Printed in the United States of America

INTRODUCTION

I like to fly fish in the salt water from shore. The truth of this statement will become clear to readers of this book, but I would like to furnish you with some other facts by way of introduction. To explain the nature of fishing's attraction, fly fishing in particular, takes a little doing. In the end, you either "get it" or you don't, but, especially for my non-fishing readers, I feel compelled to try.

I have an idea that there are lots of potential fly fishers out there, lacking only exposure to the right stimuli to bring them to their true destiny. During childhood, sensitivity to these influences is high. My grandfather's boat, a leaky flat-bottomed affair reached by a dock reminiscent of a balance beam, took me out for initiation into the angler's world. Our quarry: winter flounder, hauled up by my father and me on hand lines, hooks baited with sand worms or night crawlers. This was heady stuff for a five-year-old. Sensing an interest, my Uncle Sonny presented me with a "real" fishing rod: six feet of fiberglass with a French spinning reel. It may have been the first thing I owned that wasn't a "toy." He intimated that I should fish for stripers, striped bass (the old timers would pronounce that as stri'-ped bass). With the Thames River down the hill from our house I could practice easily.

This isn't exactly true, but my sister and I like to say we lived at New London's Ocean Beach all summer. We certainly spent a lot of time there, my mother in her beach chair, engrossed in a murder mystery novel, and our cousins along as playmates. More often than not I could be found floating face down in the water, my trusty mask and snorkel allowing uninterrupted investigation of the sandy bottom. I spent so many hours at this that, every so often, my mother would check behind my ears for gills. Observing small bait fish and their behavior, I would on occasion bump face to face into a striped bass looking for lunch.

When I was introduced to fly fishing by my college art professor, a new world opened up. In a selfless and no doubt much regretted burst of generosity, my wife traded some antique fishing lures once belonging to her grandfather for a new fly fishing outfit for me. Targeting local trout streams of mediocre quality and with little success, I turned to the salt water with this tackle and never looked back. This was the 1970's and a fly caster on the beach was a very unusual sight. I loved everything about it. First of all, the casting itself was a challenge. Done right, there is a graceful efficiency to the back and forth motion wherein the caster uses the weight of the line, not the lure, to fire out a cast. It just takes practice, along with a rudimentary sense of timing and physics to get proficient. It takes a long time to encounter and master all the variables.

The flies themselves are an attraction. They are tied by using thread and adhesives to mount materials such as feathers, fur, buck tail, tinsel and various synthetic fibers to hooks so that, in some way, they resemble a food item to a predator fish. In fresh water angling, they are usually fabricated to look like insects (flies). For saltwater they most often mimic small bait fish. The ability to identify these small creatures in the water can aid the angler in choosing which deception to use. I tie all my flies and take great pleasure in doing so. Nearly all are based on basic patterns developed by well known pioneers of the sport: Lefty Kreh's Deceiver, Bob Clouser's Minnow, Joe Brook's Blonde and Bob Popovic's epoxy creations. Every fly tier I know puts his or her own spin on things, though, and variations are endless. I like to make my flies aesthetically satisfying, even if they are to be chewed to pieces by a savage bluefish. The flies illustrated in this book are all of the type used in the photograph on the facing page and simulate the primary prey of the predators present at that time.

Fishing from shore: you in your environment, the fish in his. That seems how it should be, on the seam between two worlds. Unlike in a stream, the fish has almost unlimited mobility. This forces one to understand what might draw a fish near shore and when that might happen. Low light often helps. For tactical reasons as well as work schedule and personal biorhythms, many of the trips illustrated in this book are in the evening or at night, when fish are less wary of shallow water. Food sources and seasons play into the equation as well. The force of the tide will sweep bait fish into certain areas as well as affect water depth. Seasonal migrations, spawning, and habitat preference will all dictate bait location and hence predator behavior.

The uncertainty of exactly what you will catch in saltwater and how big it will be adds excitement to the game: stripers, bluefish, weakfish, shad. In the warmest water of late summer, bonito, false albacore, spanish mackerel, ladyfish, jacks, and even small bluefin tuna can be found in our inshore waters. And what of the stripers? They might be anything from 6 ounces to 60 pounds!

This book is about familiarity and home waters, but also the continual pleasure of surprise. The subjects form a visual diary of places I fish. No location pictured is more than 30 minutes by car from my home in Mystic, Connecticut; most are no more than 15. Southeastern Connecticut's and Southwestern Rhode Island's shores are a rich complex of beaches, coves, rivers, and bays. Fishing it well requires that you slow down, observe with heightened sensitivity, and maintain a curious nature. You will be rewarded by the application of the knowledge you acquire. The start of every outing holds the possibility of adventure. With the first cast its easy to disappear into a moving meditation in which the everyday world slips away.

I would like to say that no fish were harmed in the creation of this book. To be truthful, I can't. I know more than one angler who is somewhat conflicted on this point. If you love these creatures so much, how can you stick them with hooks and torture them on a line? I do my best to minimize stress to the fish. There are some scientists who would maintain that fish do not feel pain in the conventional sense of higher order mammals. I don't know. Sharp hooks with flattened barbs make for an easy release. A lip-hooked striper does not bleed, but sure is anxious to get back to the water. Already I think I "doth protest too much." I release them all. The hunter gene demands expression, and there's no denying 500,000 years of human experience.

Now, about the photographs: they are landscapes with an angler. At the inspired suggestion of my ever-patient wife Mary, I decided to combine the two interests that absorb much of my dedication and effort: landscape photography and fly fishing. I wanted to maintain the documentary style of my art and suggest both the mundane and sublime moments of fishing. Selected from a larger group, originally titled *Fly Fishing for Striped Bass*, they were taken over the course of three years but have been and ordered to produce a single composite one for this book.

Since I often fish alone, I am the angler in each photograph. A camera mounted on a tripod, tripped by a delay timer, was used. I would set up the composition, plan my location in the frame, and then ran like heck to arrive in time to be fishing when the shutter clicked. In the many cases where long exposures were used in low light (some range upwards of 40 minutes), I opened the shutter and simply ran into the scene, fished for the required exposure time, and returned to camera to close the shutter. In these, the back and forth trip to the camera does not show because I was moving quickly and the transit time compared in proportion to the overall exposure was nil. In some, the figure is somewhat transparent because the moments of transition allowed enough light to strike the film from the background. On rare occasions I had a helper who could trip the shutter after all was in place. The figure blurs slightly in the long exposures, and a moving fly rod will show in only the shortest ones.

The facing page of each image contains a description of the conditions at the time the photograph was taken. Location, date, wind, and moon phase are listed along with the primary prey species present. Also included is an e-mail report, sent to a group of fellow fly fishing enthusiasts as way of sharing information and experience. They were a way to relive the trip, as well as a record that could be consulted in future seasons. The informal nature of the writing is something I hope the reader will forgive. I have gone back into them to correct spelling and improve the comprehension of these rapidly composed messages, but wanted to maintain the spontaneity. The e-mails relate to the place of the photograph, but may have been written the following days. I picked them based on interest, and therefore they may not represent fairly the day-to-day experience of fishing, which would include many more unremarkable reports. A map follows with the locations of each plate.

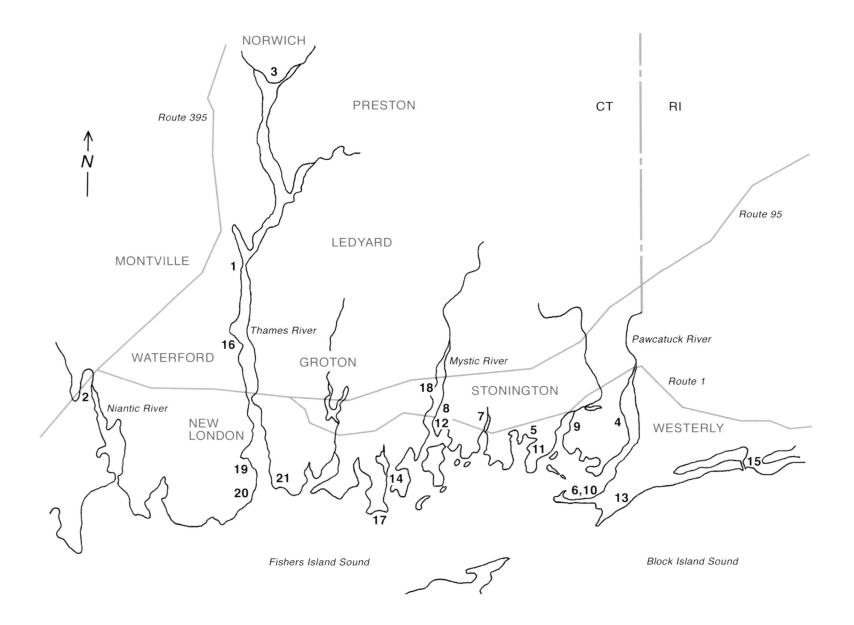

NORWICH

PRESTON

CT   RI

Route 395

↑
N
—

3

MONTVILLE

LEDYARD

Route 95

1

Thames River

16

WATERFORD

GROTON

Mystic River

Pawcatuck River

18

STONINGTON

Route 1

2

Niantic River

NEW
LONDON

8

7

12

5

9

4

WESTERLY

11

19

21

15

14

6,10

20

13

17

Fishers Island Sound

Block Island Sound

THAMES RIVER

Date: 1 January

Tide: mid outgoing

Wind: light NW

Moon: first quarter

Prey species: striped killifish, *Fundulus majalis*

To: Fishing report list
Date: 1 Jan 7:31:43 PM US/Eastern
Subject: Starting out right

First off, the best New Year's wishes to all. In what is becoming a tradition, my neighbor Bruce and I decided to shake off the night before's celebration with a fresh air expedition to the Thames in search of the year's first striped bass. We ended up in what (I have to admit) is probably the world's ugliest place to fish. But you know the saying, one of the great pillars of angling wisdom: fish where the fish are. The warm water outflow attracts them, a hot tub for freezing stripers. At the shore, I bent down to pick up what we called as kids a lucky stone, the kind with a single white stripe: a good sign.

Amid the drift wood, floating Styrofoam cups and oil booms we made our casts: sink tip line to get down near the pilings and a Clouser Minnow to dance a seductive jig. It didn't take long; we each landed a small striper in the 14 in. range and beat a retreat back to the car to warm our fingers. Sun broke through the clouds as we left, and I thought of those fish as a small deposit on a bright new season to come. Cheers!

1

NIANTIC RIVER

Date: 12 February

Tide: low incoming

Wind: light W

Moon: third quarter

Prey species: mummichogs, *Fundulus heteroclitis*

To: Fishing report list
Date: 15 Feb 6:42:39 PM US/Eastern
Subject: Success by small degrees

Well, with this late "January" thaw, I fished nearly every day this week, looking for a striper or the elusive sea run brown trout I have yet to catch. I'm happy as long as ice doesn't freeze up the guides of the rod: that's a good day for February. At the Golden Spur of the Niantic River, I tried high water (AM), low water (after work), just a bit each day, about 45 min. to an hour each time. I did not catch a striper or a sea run. I did see a sea run though, and miracle of miracles, it grabbed at my fly, and I felt and saw the strike (well, a small tug is more accurate). The little guy was shy, I guess. Anyway, it's an improvement on a swirl, which is all I've had so far... I will take success by small degrees, and who knows, maybe even catch one some day.

2

THAMES RIVER

Date: 29 March

Tide: mid outgoing

Wind: calm

Moon: waning gibbous

Prey species: alewives, *Alosa pseudoharengus*

smelt, *Osmerus mordax*

To: Fishing report list
Date: 30 Mar 12:03:15 AM US/Eastern
Subject: Too slow, too deep...

In an effort to shake off the winter cobwebs, I decided to head out to Norwich harbor Friday afternoon to give the old arm a shake-down session. Gulls were lazily dipping down to the water, and some just sat in the current. Throwing a big herring-style fly and super-fast sinking line, I repeated the cold water mantra: slow and deep, slow and deep...

A tremendous weight fell upon the line. Wow, this is it, I thought, that 25 pounder that's been waiting for me all winter, the one I saw in a dream during the February blizzard. But it didn't move, not a bit. It was hung up on some unseen obstacle; I pulled, changed angles, pulled again. Nothing doing... I really yanked, POP. Fly: gone, leader: gone, first 5 feet of fly line: gone. That's too slow, too deep.

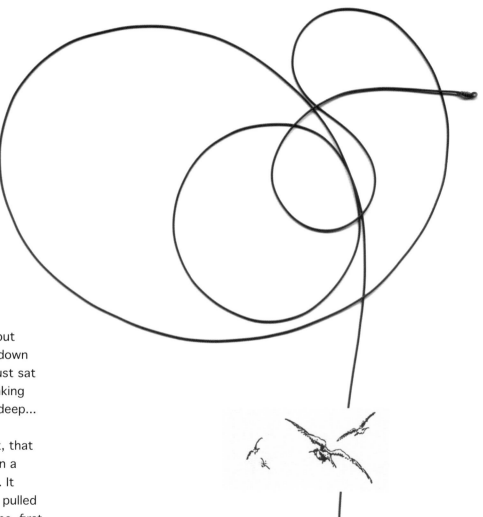

3

PAWCATUCK RIVER

Date: 28 April

Tide: low outgoing

Wind: calm

Moon: waxing crescent

Prey species: mummichaugs, *Fundulus heteroclitus*

To: Fishing report list
Date: 29 Apr 12:39:42 PM US/Eastern
Subject: Bruised knuckles, or, baby, it hurts so good

It is refreshing to file a fishing AND catching report finally.
Things are slowly picking up in the Pawcatuck River, was out
last night in the fog, caught three fish in a brief span. The first
was a feisty 18 in., next a 14 in. and then a 12 in. specimen.
I was almost afraid to catch a fourth at that descending rate.

Caught the last of the outgoing tide on the Mystic River on the
way home. Scoped out a bridge outflow and thought I saw a
swirl but wasn't sure. I waited a minute then tried a few drifts
through the area. A tap on the line-- I set the hook and felt
a powerful surge. My drag was set for schoolies, and the reel
spun like crazy, the handle rapping my knuckles with a staccato
beat. Ouch! But I was smiling nonetheless, of course. It was last
December since I had seen such a nice fish, clean and bright,
about 26 in.

4

STONINGTON

Date: 4 May

Tide: low outgoing

Wind: light E

Moon: waning gibbous

Prey species: undetermined

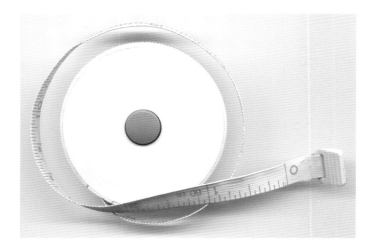

To: Fishing report list
Date: 5 May 1:03:56 AM US/Eastern
Subject: Bass @ $1.25 an inch

My habit of sneaking in any opportune moment for a piscatorial fix is well known to this list. With a moment to kill Sunday afternoon, I shared a bridge outflow with another angler, whose patience was impressive until one of my casts came a little too close, and he/she flew away. Not much doing on top, I switched to a heavy Clouser and began some slow swings down deep. Wow, I thought, this is a heavy fly, I snagged the bottom already! A sharp tug on the line and the bottom started to move! Line peeled from the reel as the crazy fish swam upstream back under the bridge and into the cove above.

Fly line is pretty tough stuff, it turns out. As it dragged and scuffed against the concrete, I was half hoping the fish would come off. At several points in this contest of wills, graphite, and nylon, I pondered the wisdom of continuing this battle, but now I was in the thick of it. The question of "who had who?" came to mind. At that particular moment, the answer wasn't terribly clear. Well, in the end human perseverance and the engineers of Trilene Big Game won the day. The fish (taped at 32 in.) was released. The big loser was the shredded fly line from a box marked $40.00, surrendered to the trash man. I figure that's striper at $1.25 an inch....

NAPATREE BEACH

Date: 30 May

Tide: mid outgoing

Wind: calm

Moon: waxing crescent

Prey species: sand eels, *Ammodytes americanus*

To: Fishing report list
Date: 31 May 11:58:19 PM US/Eastern
Subject: Warm night, cool jazz, hot bass

Picture this:
Two nights before as you reeled up for the night, a huge bass nails the fly and thrashes a 4 foot spray of water into the night air. It trashes your tippet, and you are left shaking at the edge of the water.

Two nights later you are back. It's calm to the point of glassy, and the stars reflect as dancing points of light on the water. The crescent moon slides towards the horizon. You are out swinging some fly line. You should probably be at a friend's dinner party, but the meeting you were at was just long enough to make plausible an excuse about not wanting to show up late. Across on the other shore, a party is getting under way in someone's back yard, live jazz band. It's cool, it's floating through the warm air. You've been practicing to throw a long line with your six weight using bigger flies than you have a right to expect. The rhythms are right, the line sails. Maybe the music helps...

Then the fish hits and thrashes way out. It's big and it's a war. You think, as the backing slips through the guides, "how sweet is this?"

6

STONINGTON

Date: 1 June

Tide: mid outgoing

Wind: light NW

Moon: first quarter

Prey species: grass shrimp, *Palaemonetes vulgaris*

To: Fishing report list
Date: 2 Jun 12:11:46 PM US/Eastern
Subject: Shedding some light on it

There were the fish just as expected. The stripers frequently set up in this outflow as dark descended. In years past, early June was a reliable time to find them feeding on top with loud pops late into the night. I could usually catch a few when they started feeding, but soon they became very selective. What they were eating was a mystery and any changes of fly pattern or size did not seem to help.

Last year I wised up and brought a bright light. As I peered into the slightly stained water, I finally saw them: shrimp! Little beady eyes glowing in the light, they were nearly transparent, barely an inch long. The bass evidently had a ready supply of cocktail sauce because they were slurping them down like there was no tomorrow. That night at the vise, I worked out a pattern on a #6 hook with melted nylon mono eyes and body of ice chenille and wood duck feathers. Adding a dab of epoxy to the eyes made them catch the light and completed the effect. An upstream cast with a dead drift presentation was the key. Any detectable change in the drift of the floating line usually meant a fish had taken the tiny offering. It was like nymphing for huge trout. I found it helpful to use a 10 ft. rod to mend line and take up slack on the hook set.

They were there again this year and had a blast Wednesday night. Some of the larger fish looked downright embarrassed with that little fly in their mouths. Even tried a dropper rig with two flies and caught several doubles.

MYSTIC RIVER

Date: 9 June

Tide: mid outgoing

Wind: calm

Moon: third quarter

Prey species: cinder worms, *Nereis limbata*

To: Fishing report list
Date: 10 Jun 10:56:04 AM US/Eastern
Subject: Stick in the mud

The wise fisherman moves around, I was told. Don't get in the habit of fishing the same spots at the same times, investigate and learn. Sounds like simple enough advice, but still, after many fishless trips, I find myself wondering what went wrong. Since the fish are never in the wrong place, that only leaves one sad conclusion. Still, sometimes you get it right, even when you don't expect it.

It was not a classic moon phase for it but, nonetheless, a heavy worm hatch in the Mystic River seaport/cemetery area Sunday night. I spotted it completely by luck, and fished some spots I have passed by for years thinking there could be no fish there in low water. Fishing with my six weight, got a 26 in. and a 30 in. along with numerous fish in the 14-18 in. range. Red Marabou Worms were producing. I almost became a permanent navigation marker in the river as muck sucked me into position. Visions of the quicksand scene in Tarzan movies darted through my brain... Help! It was actually scary for a few minutes. Boots were freed up only after much difficulty and with great relief.

STONINGTON

Date: 13 June

Tide: high slack

Wind: calm

Moon: waning crescent

Prey species: mummichaugs, *Fundulus heteroclitus*

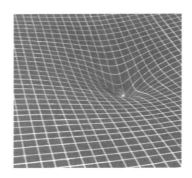

To: Fishing report list
Date: 14 Jun 5:44:07 PM US/Eastern
Subject: Fishing around

Taking advantage of good evening tides last week, I found good but not spectacular fishing. Still, I'll take it. Moving around seemed like a good plan. Napatree at last light was the most consistent. I heard about weakfish there, too. Quiambaug, Mystic River, and Mason's Island all had a few modest fish.

Tried the marshes around Barn Island several nights. Action slower than earlier in the season, but one calm and misty evening I waded out to the edge of the submerged spartina grass bank. As the fog slid in, I lost sight of the shore behind me. A slight brightening of the sky directly overhead placed me in a silvery void. As many of you know, I am easily given over to distraction by such matters. I speculated on the fact that, except for the anchoring effect of gravity, I could very well believe that I had been transported to another dimension of time and space. A firm jolt to my rod brought me back to matters at hand. A solid striper that wanted nothing more than to get from that shallow water to Fisher's Island as fast as possible!

NAPATREE BEACH

Date: 15 June

Tide: high incoming

Wind: light SW

Moon: new

Prey species: sand eels, *Ammodytes americanus*

To: Fishing report list
Date: 16 Jun 10:56:03 AM US/Eastern
Subject: Light show/no show

Went out to Napatree last night on a promising tide, although that persistent flashing off to the north was worrisome. Started casting, working down the backside beach toward the West. On the way out I picked up a pottery shard, a remnant of the houses and lives swept away from this sand spit by the '38 hurricane, otherwise it was very quiet. As I got near the salt pond, the flashes began to intensify from the southwest, moving toward me. Maybe it will stay south? It soon became a little too scary and rain started to splatter. Clearing out looked like the wise thing to do, a decision made easier by the "no show" on the stripers' part. I thought fishing was supposed to be good as a front approaches...

Back at the car, I could see intense flashes to the south, but couldn't get the full effect with the view blocked by the dune and beach cabanas. Drove down to the Watch Hill lighthouse (ah, a clear vista) and was treated to the most fantastic 45-minute light show imaginable. Bolts, streaks, and spider webs of lightning ripped through the southern sky. Left any Napatree bass for another night.

LIGHTNING CASUALITES
BY STATE 1959-1994

STONINGTON

Date: 6 July

Tide: low outgoing

Wind: light S

Moon: third quarter

Prey species: undetermined

To: Fishing report list
Date: 7 Jul 12:37:28 AM US/Eastern
Subject: Summer slam: a new perspective

Sometimes it just takes a reorientation of perspective to help define an interesting trip. I just had to wet a line last night after the rounds of family picnics and get-togethers during the holiday weekend. Last year I made the mistake of going out to Napatree on the 4th of July and was greeted with an armada of boats anchored along the shore. No thanks!

Found some quieter waters at a bridge outflow in Stonington. There were hickory shad blitzing (do hickory shad blitz?) some small unseen bait. Experimented with several small flies, with limited success. Switching back to the small Clousers that always seem to work with shad, I started hooking up: first a shad, then a small striper, another shad, another shad and then a small bluefish. Another shad got suckered and then a small weakfish. Wow! I'm calling it an early summer grand slam: four species in less than an hour. Too bad the largest was only 14 inches.

MYSTIC RIVER

Date: 2 August

Tide: mid outgoing

Wind: calm

Moon: waning gibbous

Prey species: immature silversides, *Menidia menidia*

To: Fishing report list
Date: 3 Aug 1:51:03 PM US/Eastern
Subject: Almost skunked again, or the thing about low pressure
        systems

Well, the deal with John is you really want him to catch fish because he's having such a good time even NOT catching fish that it's hard to resist thinking about what would happen if he did get some nice action. Low pressure was giving us a pretty difficult night to deal with; I figured that maybe Napatree would give us a chance for some fish. But no, wind blowing hard from the east had us right-handers with flies buzzing our ears, even with side arm casts. At the jetty it was blowing right in our faces. No bait, no fish, things looked grim.

I felt the pressure (which was now high psychologically at least) to get a fish or two. The Mystic River had saved several trips for me recently so off we went, arriving to find a bait slinger with a 30 in. bass dead on the dock and the exciting news that he had just lost another of equal size. Things were looking up! I momentarily lost my cool and ran to rig up a huge eel fly. John patiently explored the spots that produced for him last time he fished the river, ending up on the bridge itself (watch those back casts!). I came back to my

senses and re-rigged with the small minnow fly that had been working so well the past few visits.

The thing about low pressure systems, as John explained it to me, is that they can be tricky. Once when he was fishing with Ron, there was a low pressure system spoiling the fishing on one side of the boat (the side that John was on) and not on the other (Ron's side). I could see that this one might be tricky too. The pressure looked a little less low at the end of the dock, so I motioned John to come down with me and we investigated. I took a few short casts and drifted the fly by the end of the dock: POW, a fish. Well, "POW" might be overstating it a bit, more a tug really. It was a small fish but it was a fish! I gave the spot to John, having satisfied myself that there was hope after all and that low pressure was at one end of the dock but not the other. But it was getting late, John had an appointment with some summer flounder in the morning, so we called it a night.

John's chest pack is pretty full, but if we all chip in, maybe there's room for a barometer?

WATCH HILL

Date: 21 August

Tide: high outgoing

Wind: light SW

Moon: first quarter

Prey species: silversides, *Menidia menidia*

immature bluefish, *Pomatomus saltatrix*

To: Fishing report list
Date: 21 Aug 9:37:14 PM US/Eastern
Subject: Fly fishing once removed, or a baby snapper has a bad day
twice

A family trip to East Beach at Watch Hill this afternoon offered a chance to sight fish in between building sand castles and boogie boarding. I walked down past the hotel to where the people thinned out and began searching for shadows on the sandy bottom. I also blind cast to the returns where the surf slides out in a noticeable outflow through the breakers. Found a few likely spots but was somewhat dismayed by my ability to catch only extremely small snapper blues. They couldn't have been more than 5 in. long. This often bodes ill in my modest experience, since they would presumably be smart enough not to hang around if there were any fish around big enough to make them into a meal. Anyway, after narrowly missing a beach jogger with a back cast--I got pretty shook up about this since I hate the sight of blood, either from hooks or a punch in the nose--I hooked another hapless snapper with my Deceiver. I could see this quite distinctly in the clear water. A wave backwash pulled my line outward a bit, and in the roiling water I lost sight of him momentarily, but noticed my line begin moving quickly to the right...a little too quickly for a snapper, so I instinctively pulled back on the rod and saw a nice fish flash in the now calming water. I guess this has happened to other people, but it's the first time it ever happened to me. I had a nice bass on. That snapper was sure having a bad day.

As I beached what turned out to be a 30-plus-inch striper, the problem welled up in my mind: was this fly fishing? Hadn't I really caught the bass on fly-caught bait? Hadn't someone on our list said any (expletive deleted) yahoo could catch fish dragging some food through the water? I apologized profusely to the fish before releasing it, saying I didn't normally do things like that. She said, "That's alright, it could happen to anyone," and besides, she was just glad it was a #2 stainless steel hook with a crushed barb and not a 6/0 cadmium plated job like the one that got her second cousin Rocco last week.

GROTON

Date: 10 September

Tide: high outgoing

Wind: light S

Moon: first quarter

Prey species: immature silversides, *Menidia menidia*

To: Fishing report list
Date: 11 Sept 4:55:56 PM US/Eastern
Subject: Displaced frustration, or why it's no picnic to be a hickory
       shad at Palmer Cove in September

Made the rounds a few times this week looking for false albacore from shore. The first week of September is always hit and miss at best, but after tantalizing glimpses and an ever so brief hook up, it has been all "miss". I admit it's kind of a sickness. Once the idea is set in my mind that, at least in theory, I could be catching these beasts, it pretty much takes over for a while at least.

With frustration growing every trip to the Rhode Island breachways and Pleasure Beach, I made my way after dark to Palmer Cove. There, to be had every night, were hickory shad in great numbers. Now, it's a pretty lowly fish in comparison, but its three great advantages are quantity, predictability, and a willingness to be caught. None of which can be said for False Albacore fished from shore. Last fall I figured out a little Clouser-type fly that would catch these guys, heavily weighted and on a #6 hook. This week I worked through

HICKORY SHAD POMOLOBUS MEDIOCRIS

experiment to develop a method of fishing it that would catch fish consistently. By last night I had satisfied myself that after 50 or 60 fish I had in fact worked it out. Every 30 seconds or so I had one on and, after a brief but energetic display of protest against my six weight fly rod, they were brought ashore and released. A few were worse for the wear, having gulped the fly so deep that their prognosis after release seemed a bit doubtful. This made me stop eventually to wonder what was I up to anyway? In "fish per hour" I was racking up the score, that's for sure. I hoped it wasn't that I was just taking out my frustrations on the poor shad...

Then it slowly dawned on me. I was building up a surplus of fish measured against time spent fishing that would be used soon enough on the Great False Albacore Wait: the hours spent blind casting, standing around waiting expectantly for the fish that sometimes shows and sometimes doesn't. I know at least a few of you know what I mean. It was some kind of psychological account that had to be balanced, funny how the mind works. Self analysis complete, I returned to the car with the tattered shreds of my sanity.

WEEKAPAUG

Date: 2 October

Tide: high incoming

Wind: strong changing to moderate SW

Moon: waning crescent

Prey species: mullet, *Mugil cepalus*

silversides, *Menidia menidia*

To: Fishing report list
Date: 3 Oct 12:13:32 AM US/Eastern
Subject: Fat Albert

Things looked bad, I got out of work at quarter to five; the wind twisted trees looked like modern dancers on a bad trip. When one has the albie affliction, these things matter not. "If I go like hell, I can get in at least an hour of good tide before it gets too dark," I thought. Off I go. On my favorite jetty, the wind was blowing so hard, I had to lean into it just to stand up. Once I nearly fell on my face when the velocity fell momentarily. Big gusts nearly took my breath away. The water was foamy with blowing spray, but I could see a school of bait; it looked like mullet. I decided to give it try. How chapped can you get in another 45 minutes?

The bait sprayed from the water; was that a boil? I began flailing the line out; the best I could do was 8 or 10 feet from the rocks, and that only between gusts. Two or three spin guys on the other side looked skeptically at my struggling efforts. Even I began to doubt the sense in this as the wind drove the fly line back at me in an automatic retrieve after touchdown on the choppy surface. Then a flash and a powerful pull: Holy cow! As line screamed from the reel and bellied into an arc from the pressure of the wind, I hopped after the running fish. It pulled so much harder than the last couple of false albacore this week, I knew it was a better fish. Sometimes it pays to be crazy.

As the sun sank below the horizon, the wind calmed. I retreated to shelter inside of the bridge and probed among the rocks for bass. Cool down...

THAMES RIVER

Date: 31 October

Tide: high outgoing

Wind: light W

Moon: waning gibbous

Prey species: silversides, *Menidia menidia*

To: Fishing report list
Date: 1 Nov 9:21:53 PM US/Eastern
Subject: Trick or Treat

Out mostly at night this Halloween week, haunting the coves and outlets in Stonington and Groton. Had a couple of great sessions with hickories at Palmers Cove. After John's report on the Thames with Ron, I decided to visit some boyhood spots from my misspent youth growing up by the Coast Guard Academy and Riverside Park. I was rewarded Friday with some great non-stop action before the sun set, small bass to 20 in. but fat and beautiful with dark backs, silvery sides and tough personalities. It was reassuring that spots I remembered from 40 years back once again hold willing fish in good numbers. It was also reassuring that I could remember the spots. In a small cove across from the sub base, I cast to swirling stripers who charged my fly, leaving a wake like a mini torpedo in the flat calm water.

GROTON LONG POINT

Date: 7 November

Tide: mid outgoing

Wind: light N

Moon: first quarter

Prey species: silversides, *Menidia menidia*

To: Fishing report list
Date: 7 Nov 10:12:46 PM US/Eastern
Subject: Small and ugly bass

Poked around today to see what was up; the weather was a darn sight more cooperative and I bet some of you are out tonight. Weekapaug Beach and Breachway both a had a fair number of small bass, but the ones at the Breachway were nearly all affected by that disturbing disease that makes white scuzz on their bodies and seems to destroy their fins. I bet 75% had some kind of problem. I got grossed out and left just as a bunch of surfers took to the waves with their boards. Went to Ocean Beach, where the water was still pretty high. Hit a half a dozen more small ones at the creek, but again, 5 had the same problem... I almost thought I was catching the same fish over and over again (maybe I was!). Perhaps they hang around together because the others are always making fun of them and they need a support group for therapy. What an ignominious fate for a noble beast. I'm sure their souls were pure despite the disfigurement.

Stopped by Groton Long Point on the way home at last light. In the serene glow I found no fish, but it hardly mattered, a landscape to balance the day. When I got home I felt sort of funny about all those fish and washed my hands twice.

MYSTIC RIVER

Date: 8 November

Tide: low outgoing

Wind: strong S

Moon: waning crescent

Prey species: immature menhaden, *Brevootia tyrannus*

To: Fishing report list
Date: 9 Nov 1:11:10 AM US/Eastern
Subject: Blown out

Ran into some hickory shad earlier in the week at Palmer Cove, including the most energetic member of the species I have yet encountered, which isn't saying that much, I grant you. It actually took some line and moved the drag (no, it didn't get into the backing) and made some spectacular jumps. Must have been high on something or one of those steroid junkies. I tried there again tonight but was blown off the water by a stiff South wind.

I found some shelter up the Mystic River under the 95 bridge. The water was filled with baby bunker [menhaden] and there were a few stripers and harbor blues harassing them. Casting to the edge of the schools got a few takers but in general very hard to hook up with so many bait fish and so few predators on them. Stayed longer than I should while the late night truckers rumbled along above me. Hard to reconcile the two worlds, but the strange amalgam of stillness and motion had its own fascination.

THAMES RIVER

Date: 15 November

Tide: mid outgoing

Wind: light NW

Moon: full

Prey species: immature menhaden, *Brevootia tyrannus*

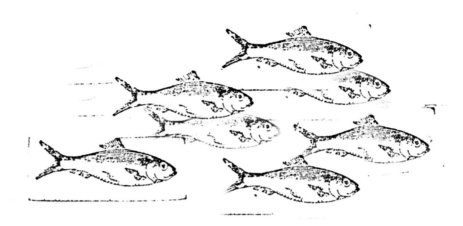

To: Fishing report list
Date: 16 Nov 11:11:58 PM US/Eastern
Subject: Boogie nights… got to keep on dancin'

Friday night held some social commitments and an uncooperative weather forecast, so I did not get out. Saturday night fever descended on me around high tide last night, so off I went. Tried a few casts in some local coves that came up unanswered. "The fish are in New London," I said to myself, "what am I doing here?" The night was cold, but the lack of wind made it quite comfortable fishing.

As I pulled up past the biker bar, I had the old disco song "Boogie Nights" blaring on the car radio. My head bobbing to the infectious beat, I was probably a curious sight with my fingerless gloves, polar fleece helmet and chest pack on. Then again, maybe I fit right in with the bar's Saturday night clientele, just now arriving for a night out at about 11:00 PM. As I let the song play to the end, I thought about years back when the biker bar was a popular dance club, back in the

days of disco. There was an innocence to that time, a kind of beautiful simplicity, dancing purely in the moment, purely for the joy of movement to the beat.

I found my spot, still well within earshot of the bar, which, by the way, was hopping this particular night. Tight schools of baby bunker swam under the light, congregated for safety. Was it my imagination that they shifted direction in choreographed unison to the beat of a live rock band at the bar?

First cast: fish on, second cast: fish on, stripers flashed, competing to get my fly. As the door of the bar opened and closed, the music alternated between a muffled din and a raucous roar. An occasional snow flurry punctuated the dark sky. I was purely in the moment, fishing purely for the joy of catching these wonderful fish in this unlikely gestalt. They were small but it didn't matter. I didn't stop until the fish did, around 12:30.

THAMES RIVER

Date: 20 November

Tide: low outgoing

Wind: moderate W

Moon: waning gibbous

Prey species: silversides, *Menidia menidia*

herring, *Alosa aestivalis*

To: Fishing report list
Date: 20 Nov 9:54:24 PM US/Eastern
Subject: Bookends

Went down to Pequot Ave. along the Thames for an early lunch hour. This to me means fishing, not eating, time. Heck, I can snack on the ride down! Took up position for a casting session from a rocky point and watched thousands of birds between the Ledge Light and Avery Point bomb the water. I hope Charlie was out there in his boat; his rod would have been bent all afternoon I bet. Another slightly smaller group of birds (maybe only a thousand or so) worked a half mile off Ocean Beach. Spent about a half hour dragging the fly through empty water, giving a reflexive sigh every once in while as I gazed at the frenzy offshore. Just about to give up, I saw a gannet wheel by (good news, the herring must be arriving!). Immediately I hooked up to a little nicer fish than I have been getting, about 22 in. OK, I can go back to work now.

When my last class ended and all questions were answered, I hurried into the car for a sunset repeat. Perched on the same rock, I again spend 30 min. casting in the gathering darkness. Switched over to a big black and blue Deceiver. Bang! A fat and sassy 24 in. striper that demanded to be played off the reel, I like that. On the way home for dinner I thought of those fish as two bright silvery bookends to an afternoon at work.

GROTON

Date: 12 December

Tide: low outgoing

Wind: moderate SW

Moon: first quarter

Prey species: herring, *Alosa aestivalis*

sand eels, *Ammodytes americanus*

To: Fishing report list
Date: 13 Dec 8:15:26 PM US/Eastern
Subject: Still out there

Busy times have kept me offline, but not from finding a little time to sneak in some fishing. The last good days were a week ago. A mild Sunday had the quality edge with 4 nice fish taken at Waterford beach, low incoming tide late afternoon, 28 in., 26 in., and two 24 in. Friday had the quantity. Twenty-five fish in an hour and a half, but all 14-16 in. at Ocean Beach, outgoing tide. Things have quieted down this week, got a couple of fish this afternoon in the snow along Pequot Ave. after being skunked last night at Ocean Beach. I struck out at the Montville Power Plant Monday. Eastern Point in Groton provided one striper after work Tuesday on a herring fly. From the forecasts the weather looks like it is deteriorating, and the water temps are falling out front along the beaches. Sigh... It seems like the reality of winter's approach has finally sunk in.

Rest has a peaceful effect on your
physical and emotional health.
Lucky Numbers 4, 8, 10, 13, 41, 42

ACKNOWLEDGMENTS

This project would not have started without the suggestion of my wife, Mary, to "do something productive with all this fishing." For this, as well as her patience and understanding, this work is dedicated to her.

Thanks are due to my photography mentors, most especially William E. Parker, whose depth of intellectual enthusiasm for the medium was infectious to this college student and whose help and encouragement over the years has been invaluable. Joyce Brodsky, Harry Callahan, John Craig, and David Kelly are all teachers who by example and demand helped the growth of my photographic work.

My angling adventures have been enhanced by many. For introducing me to fly fishing, I have to thank Roy Superior, terror to trout everywhere. For his pioneering book on saltwater fly fishing, as well as never to be forgotten casting instruction, thanks to Bernard "Lefty" Kreh. Thanks to Alan Caolo and Ron Whiteley for generously sharing locations and techniques over the years. Members of Conn/RI Costal Fly Fishers have been fishing partners, friends, and advisors over the years, by which I have been greatly enriched. My breachway buddies, especially the founding members of Albacore Anonymous (you know who you are) have provided companionship and good humor, making each September into a much anticipated reunion.

Pressed into the role of photographic assistants, no complaints were heard from fishing companions and friends Gay Myers and Bruce Vandal, or my daughter Karli Hendrickson, who I tried hard to infect with the fishing bug. She patiently endured.

Family, friends, and colleagues who have put up with various and sundry inconveniences due to my obsessive angling involvements, please forgive, even though, no doubt, I don't deserve it.

In the production of this book, I have benefited from the ministrations of many individuals. Andrea Wollensak graciously advised on design and production. Mark Braunstein and Brett Terry provided valuable technical consultations. Tom Couser and Janis Mink generously read copy, struggling to save me from grammatical and syntactical errors and embarrassing misspellings. Bob McKenna of Flat Hammock Press was encouraging all the way through and gave me unlimited design and content freedom. Also, thanks to Stephen Jones and Greta Jones of Flat Hammock for their support of this project.   - *TH*